100

HOLLYWOOD'S

BEST

MOTIVATIONAL

QUOTES

FROM THE GREATEST FILMS OF ALL TIME

Literary Muse

FAQ'S ABOUT THIS BOOK

WHAT IS THE PURPOSE OF THIS BOOK?

The book aims to inspire and motivate readers through a collection of impactful quotes from various movies and series. Each quote is accompanied by its meaning to provide deeper insight and encouragement.

HOW ARE THE QUOTES SELECTED?

Quotes are chosen based on their motivational and inspirational value. They come from a wide range of movies and series, ensuring diversity in themes and messages.

HOW CAN I USE THIS BOOK EFFECTIVELY?

Read the quotes and their meanings to find motivation and inspiration. Reflect on how the messages apply to your own life and challenges. You can also use the quotes as daily affirmations or share them with others.

ARE THE QUOTES ORGANIZED IN ANY PARTICULAR WAY?

The quotes are presented in a way that each stands alone with its accompanying explanation. There is no specific order, allowing readers to browse and find quotes that resonate with them at any given moment.

HOW CAN I SHARE MY FEEDBACK ABOUT THE BOOK?

Feedback can be shared through the publisher's website or by leaving a review on the platform where the book was purchased. The author appreciates and values reader feedback to improve future editions.

HOW CAN I SHARE MY FEEDBACK ABOUT THE BOOK?

Yes, the author plans to continue exploring motivational themes and may release additional volumes focusing on different sources or themes. Keep an eye out for announcements about new releases.

YODA (VOICED BY FRANK OZ)

"DO, OR DO NOT. THERE IS NO TRY."

STAR WARS: EPISODE V - THE
EMPIRE STRIKES BACK

MEANING:

This quote emphasizes the importance of commitment and decisiveness. It suggests that attempting something with a half-hearted effort is not truly trying. True effort involves full dedication to either doing something or not doing it at all. It's a call to commit fully to one's actions rather than making excuses.

"ONE OFTEN MEETS HIS DESTINY ON THE ROAD HE TAKES TO AVOID IT."

KUNG FU PANDA

MEANING:

This quote suggests that despite our efforts to avoid certain paths or outcomes, we often end up encountering them anyway. It highlights the idea that destiny has a way of finding us, regardless of the actions we take to sidestep it. Ultimately, it speaks to the inevitability of certain life events and the importance of accepting and embracing our journey, even if it leads us to places we initially tried to avoid.

MEANING:

This quote highlights the importance of actions over internal qualities or intentions. It suggests that a person's true character is revealed through their behavior and choices. People are judged by their actions, which have a tangible impact, rather than their hidden qualities or thoughts. It emphasizes the value of outward conduct and tangible contributions.

MEANING:

This quote encourages persistence and resilience in the face of challenges. It suggests that progress and growth come from continual effort and not giving up. Even when facing obstacles, it's important to maintain forward momentum. It's a reminder to stay focused on the future and keep striving towards goals.

NICHOLAS SPARKS (BOOK), VOICED
BY MANDY MOORE (AS JAMIE
SULLIVAN)

"YOU CAN'T LIVE YOUR LIFE FOR OTHER PEOPLE. YOU'VE GOT TO DO WHAT'S RIGHT FOR YOU, EVEN IF IT HURTS SOME PEOPLE YOU LOVE."

A WALK TO REMEMBER

MEANING:

This quote underscores the importance of authenticity and self-fulfillment. It suggests that while it's natural to care about others' opinions, ultimately, one must make decisions based on their own values and desires. Sometimes, pursuing what's right for oneself may disappoint or hurt others, but personal integrity and happiness should take precedence. It encourages living true to oneself.

BRAD PITT

"OUR LIVES ARE DEFINED BY OPPORTUNITIES, EVEN THE ONES WE MISS."

THE CURIOUS CASE OF BENJAMIN BUTTON

MEANING:

This quote reflects on the significant role that opportunities play in shaping our lives. Both the opportunities we seize and those we let pass by influence our paths and personal growth. It suggests that missed opportunities are also valuable, as they can lead to new directions and lessons. It's a reminder to recognize and learn from all opportunities, whether taken or missed.

MEANING:

This quote emphasizes the power of belief and positive thinking in achieving extraordinary goals. It suggests that without believing in the possibility of success, one cannot accomplish great things. Confidence and faith in oneself are crucial components of overcoming challenges and achieving what seems impossible. It encourages a mindset of possibility and optimism.

"HAPPINESS CAN BE FOUND EVEN IN THE DARKEST OF TIMES, IF ONE ONLY REMEMBERS TO TURN ON THE LIGHT."

HARRY POTTER AND THE PRISONER
OF AZKABAN

MEANING:

This quote suggests that even in the most difficult and challenging times, happiness is possible if one makes the effort to find it. It encourages a proactive approach to seeking positivity and light amidst darkness. By focusing on the positive and taking action to create joy, one can overcome negative circumstances. It emphasizes the power of perspective and personal agency in finding happiness.

"IT'S NOT OUR ABILITIES THAT SHOW WHAT WE TRULY ARE... IT IS OUR CHOICES."

HARRY POTTER AND THE CHAMBER OF SECRETS

MEANING:

This quote highlights the importance of choices over inherent abilities. It suggests that our true character is revealed through the decisions we make, rather than our natural talents or skills. Actions and choices reflect our values and define who we are. It emphasizes the significance of ethical and intentional decision-making.

MEANING:

This quote highlights the rapid pace of life and the importance of taking moments to pause and appreciate the present. It reminds us that in our busy lives, we often overlook the beauty and joy in everyday moments. By stopping to look around, we can find meaning and satisfaction in the present rather than always chasing the next goal. It's a call to mindfulness and savoring the small pleasures that life offers.

"YOUR MIND IS LIKE THIS WATER, MY FRIEND. WHEN IT IS AGITATED, IT BECOMES DIFFICULT TO SEE. BUT IF YOU ALLOW IT TO SETTLE, THE ANSWER BECOMES CLEAR."

KUNG FU PANDA

MEANING:

This quote compares the mind to water, illustrating how agitation and unrest can cloud our judgment and perception. When our thoughts are turbulent and unsettled, it becomes challenging to see things clearly and make sound decisions. This metaphor emphasizes the importance of inner peace and tranquility in understanding situations and finding solutions to problems. It suggests that taking time to relax and clear our minds can lead to better decision-making and a clearer perspective on life.

MEANING:

This quote acknowledges that the past can be painful, but it offers a choice in how to respond to it. Running from the past means avoiding or denying it, while learning from it involves facing it, understanding it, and using it as a foundation for growth. It encourages using past experiences as lessons to improve the future. It's a reminder that growth often comes from confronting and learning from past difficulties.

"ALL WE HAVE TO DECIDE IS WHAT TO DO WITH THE TIME THAT IS GIVEN TO US."

THE LORD OF THE RINGS: THE
FELLOWSHIP OF THE RING

MEANING:

This quote emphasizes the importance of making intentional choices with the limited time we have. It suggests that while we cannot control the amount of time we have, we can control how we use it. Making meaningful and purposeful decisions can lead to a fulfilling life. It's a call to focus on what we can do now, rather than worrying about things beyond our control.

"JUST KEEP SWIMMING."

FINDING NEMO

MEANING:

This quote encourages persistence and resilience in the face of challenges. It suggests that by continuing to move forward, even in difficult times, we can overcome obstacles. The simplicity of the phrase underscores the idea that sometimes, the best approach is to keep going, no matter how hard it gets. It's a reminder of the importance of perseverance.

MEANING:

This quote highlights the distinction between mere existence and truly living. It suggests that while death is inevitable, not everyone takes full advantage of life's opportunities and experiences. Truly living involves embracing life's adventures, taking risks, and pursuing one's passions. It's a call to live life fully and meaningfully.

"HOPE IS A GOOD THING, MAYBE THE BEST OF THINGS, AND NO GOOD THING EVER DIES."

MEANING:

This quote emphasizes the enduring power of hope. It suggests that hope is a fundamental and positive force that can sustain us through difficult times. Even when situations seem bleak, hope provides the strength to keep going. It's a reminder that maintaining hope can lead to positive outcomes and that its impact is timeless.

"THE JOURNEY OF A THOUSAND MILES BEGINS WITH ONE STEP."

MOVIE: THE FORBIDDEN KINGDOM

MEANING:

This quote highlights the importance of taking the first step towards achieving a goal, no matter how daunting it may seem. It suggests that all significant achievements start with a single, often small, action. By breaking down large goals into manageable steps, progress can be made. It's a reminder that the first step is crucial to embarking on any journey or undertaking.

"YOU HAVE TO DO EVERYTHING YOU CAN. YOU HAVE TO WORK YOUR HARDEST, AND IF YOU STAY POSITIVE, YOU HAVE A SHOT AT A SILVER LINING."

SILVER LININGS PLAYBOOK

MEANING:

This quote emphasizes the importance of hard work and a positive attitude in achieving success. It suggests that giving your best effort and maintaining optimism increases the chances of finding positive outcomes, even in challenging situations. By staying committed and positive, you can overcome difficulties and achieve your goals. It's a call to persistence and maintaining a hopeful outlook.

"TO INFINITY AND BEYOND!"

MEANING:

This quote encourages boundless ambition and the pursuit of limitless possibilities. It suggests that there are no limits to what one can achieve if they dare to dream big. The phrase embodies a spirit of exploration and pushing beyond conventional boundaries. It's a call to aim high and believe in the possibility of achieving the extraordinary.

"CARPE DIEM. SEIZE THE DAY, BOYS. MAKE YOUR LIVES EXTRAORDINARY."

MEANING:

This quote encourages taking advantage of the present moment and making the most out of life. It emphasizes the importance of living fully and making each day count. By seizing the day, one can create extraordinary experiences and achievements. It's a call to action to live proactively and with purpose.

"IT'S NOT THE YEARS IN YOUR LIFE THAT COUNT. IT'S THE LIFE IN YOUR YEARS."

MEANING:

This quote suggests that the quality of life is more important than the quantity of years lived. It emphasizes the significance of meaningful experiences, joy, and fulfillment. Living a rich, purposeful life is what truly matters, rather than just the passage of time. It's a reminder to focus on making each moment valuable and memorable.

"YOU MISS 100% OF THE SHOTS YOU DON'T TAKE."

THE OFFICE

MEANING:

This quote highlights the importance of taking risks and trying, even if success is not guaranteed. By not attempting, you automatically eliminate any chance of success. It encourages taking opportunities and being proactive in pursuing goals. It's a call to action to overcome fear and hesitation to maximize potential achievements.

MEANING:

This quote offers hope and reassurance during difficult times. It suggests that just when things seem most challenging, relief and positive change are imminent. The darkest moments are often followed by a new beginning or improvement. It's a reminder to stay hopeful and resilient, as better times are ahead.

"DON'T LET ANYONE EVER MAKE YOU FEEL LIKE YOU DON'T DESERVE WHAT YOU WANT."

10 THINGS I HATE ABOUT YOU

MEANING:

This quote emphasizes self-worth and the importance of not letting others undermine your aspirations. It encourages confidence and belief in your right to pursue your desires. Others' opinions should not deter you from striving for what you want. It's a call to maintain self-respect and assertiveness in the face of doubt.

"GET BUSY LIVING, OR GET BUSY DYING."

THE SHAWSHANK REDEMPTION

MEANING:

This quote highlights the urgency of actively engaging in life rather than passively letting it pass by. It suggests that one must choose to fully embrace life and its experiences. Not actively living equates to a slow decline or wasting one's potential. It's a powerful reminder to take control of your life and make it meaningful.

MEANING:

This quote speaks to the importance of self-acceptance and confidence. Over time, you realize that external judgments and labels are not as important as your own self-belief. Trusting in your true self allows you to overcome negative perceptions. It's a reminder to focus on self-worth and inner strength rather than others' opinions.

"THERE'S NO PLACE LIKE HOME."

MEANING:

This quote emphasizes the unique comfort, security, and sense of belonging that home provides. Home is often where one feels most at peace and truly themselves. It highlights the special, irreplaceable nature of one's home environment. It's a reminder of the value and significance of the place where we feel most connected.

"THE ONLY THING STANDING BETWEEN YOU AND YOUR GOAL IS THE STORY YOU KEEP TELLING YOURSELF AS TO WHY YOU CAN'T ACHIEVE IT."

MEANING:

This quote suggests that self-doubt and negative self-talk are the main obstacles to achieving goals. Changing your internal narrative to one of confidence and possibility can unlock your potential. It emphasizes the power of mindset in overcoming challenges. It's a call to reframe your thinking to support your aspirations.

"IT IS NOT OUR ABILITIES THAT SHOW WHAT WE TRULY ARE. IT IS OUR CHOICES."

HARRY POTTER AND THE CHAMBER OF SECRETS

MEANING:

This quote highlights the importance of decisions over inherent talents or skills. What defines us is the choices we make and how we act upon them. It underscores the idea that character is revealed through actions and decisions. It's a reminder that ethical and intentional choices shape our true selves.

"YOU HAVE WITHIN YOU RIGHT NOW, EVERYTHING YOU NEED TO DEAL WITH WHATEVER THE WORLD CAN THROW AT YOU."

PITCH PERFECT

MEANING:

This quote emphasizes the inner strength and resources everyone possesses. It suggests that you already have the capability to handle challenges. Trusting in your own abilities and resilience is crucial. It's a reminder of self-sufficiency and the power of self-belief in facing difficulties.

MEANING:

This quote encourages self-confidence and recognizes hidden strengths. Often, we underestimate our own abilities and potential. It's a reminder that we possess greater courage, strength, and intelligence than we realize. It inspires belief in oneself and the courage to face challenges.

"DO WHAT YOU HAVE TO DO SO YOU CAN DO WHAT YOU WANT TO DO."

THE GREAT DEBATERS

MEANING:

This quote emphasizes the importance of fulfilling responsibilities to achieve personal goals. By handling necessary tasks and obligations, you create the freedom to pursue your desires. It's a reminder that discipline and hard work pave the way for enjoying life's pleasures. It encourages a balanced approach to duty and aspiration.

MEANING:

This quote emphasizes the fundamental human experience of love. It suggests that mutual love is the most profound and valuable lesson in life. Loving and being loved enriches life and provides deep fulfillment. It's a reminder of the importance of forming meaningful, loving relationships.

"SOMETIMES IT IS THE PEOPLE WHO NO ONE IMAGINES ANYTHING OF WHO DO THE THINGS THAT NO ONE CAN IMAGINE."

MEANING:

This quote highlights the potential in overlooked individuals. Often, those underestimated or ignored achieve extraordinary things. It emphasizes the value of every person's unique potential. It's a reminder to recognize and appreciate the unexpected contributions of others.

"YESTERDAY IS HISTORY, TOMORROW IS A MYSTERY, BUT TODAY IS A GIFT. THAT IS WHY IT IS CALLED THE PRESENT."

KUNG FU PANDA

MEANING:

The quote stresses the significance of being present in the moment. It indicates that focusing on the past or future can take away from enjoying the present. By labeling today as a "gift," the quote promotes gratitude and mindfulness, highlighting the value of the current moment as a special chance to enrich our lives.

MEANING:

This quote emphasizes the importance of effort and persistence over winning. Success is found in continuous effort and striving to do your best. The true value lies in the journey and dedication, not just the outcome. It's a call to maintain perseverance and commitment in all endeavors.

MEANING:

This quote suggests that the essence of life is found in exploration, connection, and emotional experience. It encourages embracing adventure, breaking barriers, and forming deep connections. Life's purpose is in experiencing the world fully and building meaningful relationships. It's a reminder to live boldly and connect deeply with others.

MEANING:

This quote emphasizes the power of choice in defining our identities. Our actions and decisions shape who we become. It suggests that identity is not fixed but is continuously formed by our choices. It's a call to take responsibility for shaping our lives and character through conscious decisions.

"SUCCESS IS NOT FINAL, FAILURE IS NOT FATAL: IT IS THE COURAGE TO CONTINUE THAT COUNTS."

MEANING:

This quote emphasizes that success and failure are not permanent states. What truly matters is the resilience and determination to keep going despite challenges. It highlights the importance of perseverance and continuous effort. Courage to move forward, regardless of past successes or failures, is what ultimately leads to long-term achievements.

MEANING:

This quote encourages boundless dreaming and ambition. By not setting limits on your aspirations, you allow yourself to achieve more than you might have thought possible. It suggests that dreaming big can propel you further in life. The only constraints are those you impose on yourself, so it's important to dream without boundaries.

IRENE BEDARD (VOICE OF
POCAHONTAS)

"SOMETIMES THE RIGHT PATH IS NOT THE EASIEST ONE."

POCAHONTAS

MEANING:

This quote acknowledges that the best or correct choices in life often come with difficulties. It suggests that challenges and obstacles are part of making worthwhile decisions. The right path may require effort, sacrifice, and perseverance. It's a reminder that worthwhile achievements often demand hard work and resilience.

MEANING:

This quote highlights the importance of meaningful and memorable experiences over merely existing. It suggests that the quality of life is defined by extraordinary moments that leave a lasting impact. These moments are what make life truly valuable and fulfilling. It's a call to seek out and cherish experiences that bring joy and wonder.

THEODORE ROOSEVELT, QUOTED
BY CHRIS PINE

"BELIEVE YOU CAN AND YOU'RE HALFWAY THERE."

WONDER WOMAN

MEANING:

This quote emphasizes the power of self-belief in achieving goals. Confidence and a positive mindset are crucial for success. By believing in your ability to succeed, you are already on the path to achieving your goals. It underscores the importance of mental attitude in overcoming challenges and reaching aspirations.

"IT'S NOT WHETHER YOU GET KNOCKED DOWN, IT'S WHETHER YOU GET UP."

ROCKY BALBOA

MEANING:

This quote focuses on resilience and the importance of recovery from setbacks. Everyone faces difficulties and failures, but what matters most is the ability to rise again. It emphasizes that true strength lies in persistence and the determination to keep going. Success is measured by how well you recover and continue after being knocked down.

"THE BEST WAY TO PREDICT YOUR FUTURE IS TO CREATE IT."

MEANING:

This quote suggests that you have control over your future through your actions and decisions. By actively shaping your life, you can influence the outcomes and direction of your future. It emphasizes proactive behavior and taking responsibility for your destiny. Planning and working towards your goals are the best ways to ensure a desired future.

RUSSELL CROWE

"WHAT WE DO IN LIFE ECHOES IN ETERNITY."

GLADIATOR

MEANING:

This quote highlights the lasting impact of our actions. The deeds we perform during our lifetime can have long-lasting effects beyond our immediate presence. It underscores the importance of living a life of significance and integrity. Our actions, whether good or bad, can leave a lasting legacy that endures through time.

"ALL OUR DREAMS CAN COME TRUE, IF WE HAVE THE COURAGE TO PURSUE THEM."

SAVING MR. BANKS

MEANING:

This quote emphasizes the importance of courage in achieving dreams. Dreams are attainable if one is brave enough to chase them despite fears and challenges. It highlights the role of determination and boldness in turning aspirations into reality. Courage is the key to transforming dreams into accomplishments.

MEANING:

This quote stresses the importance of looking forward rather than dwelling on the past. Focusing on past mistakes or missed opportunities can prevent you from seeing new possibilities. It's a call to let go of the past and concentrate on the future. Progress and growth come from embracing what lies ahead, not what is left behind.

"YOU ARE NEVER TOO OLD TO SET ANOTHER GOAL OR TO DREAM A NEW DREAM."

THE CHRONICLES OF NARNIA: THE
LION, THE WITCH AND THE
WARDROBE

MEANING:

This quote encourages continuous aspiration and goal-setting regardless of age. It suggests that it's never too late to pursue new ambitions and dreams. Age should not be a barrier to personal growth and achievement. It promotes a mindset of lifelong learning and evolving aspirations.

MEANING:

This quote reflects confidence and self-assurance. It suggests that one's worth and actions do not need validation from others. Confidence in oneself means not needing to justify or prove anything to others. It's a declaration of self-belief and independence from external judgments.

MEANING:

This quote offers hope and optimism during tough times. It suggests that despite current difficulties, there are better things ahead. Maintaining a positive outlook can help navigate through challenges. It's a reminder that good things are possible even when the present seems bleak.

"DON'T EVER LET SOMEBODY TELL YOU YOU CAN'T DO SOMETHING. NOT EVEN ME. ALL RIGHT? YOU GOT A DREAM, YOU GOTTA PROTECT IT."

THE PURSUIT OF HAPPYNESS

MEANING:

This quote encourages protecting and pursuing your dreams despite others' doubts or discouragements. It emphasizes the importance of self-belief and perseverance. Others may not see your potential, but you must remain steadfast in your aspirations. Protecting your dreams is crucial for achieving them, regardless of external negativity.

TOM HANKS

"LIFE IS LIKE A BOX OF CHOCOLATES. YOU NEVER KNOW WHAT YOU'RE GONNA GET."

FORREST GUMP

MEANING:

This quote highlights the unpredictability and variety of life. Just like a box of chocolates with assorted flavors, life is full of unexpected events and surprises. It suggests embracing the unknown and finding joy in life's surprises. The uncertainty of life adds to its richness and excitement.

"COURAGE IS NOT THE ABSENCE OF FEAR BUT RATHER THE JUDGMENT THAT SOMETHING ELSE IS MORE IMPORTANT THAN FEAR."

A WALK TO REMEMBER

MEANING:

This quote redefines courage as acting despite fear rather than not feeling fear. True courage involves recognizing fear and choosing to prioritize what matters most. It's about making decisions based on values and goals that surpass the fear. It encourages bravery through understanding and prioritizing what truly matters.

MEANING:

This quote encourages embracing uniqueness and individuality. Conforming to fit in can suppress your true self and potential. Being different is valuable and should be celebrated. It's a call to embrace and showcase your distinctive qualities rather than hiding them to fit in.

MEANING:

This quote suggests that luck is created through actions and effort. Rather than waiting for good fortune, actively working towards goals can generate opportunities. It emphasizes personal agency and responsibility in shaping outcomes. Success often comes from taking initiative and making the most of circumstances.

CLIFF ROBERTSON

"WITH GREAT POWER COMES GREAT RESPONSIBILITY."

SPIDER-MAN

MEANING:

This quote highlights the ethical and moral obligations that come with power and influence. Those who possess power must use it wisely and for the greater good. It emphasizes accountability and the duty to act responsibly. Power should be exercised with a sense of responsibility and integrity to benefit others.

MEANING:

This quote encourages breaking free from limitations and aiming higher with your aspirations. It suggests that fear should not restrict the scope of your dreams. Dreaming big requires courage and an open mind to envision possibilities beyond the ordinary. By dreaming bigger, you allow yourself to achieve greater things and expand your potential.

"IT'S NOT ABOUT HOW HARD YOU HIT. IT'S ABOUT HOW HARD YOU CAN GET HIT AND KEEP MOVING FORWARD."

ROCKY BALBOA

MEANING:

This quote highlights the importance of resilience and perseverance. Life's challenges and setbacks are inevitable, but true strength lies in the ability to endure and continue despite difficulties. It's not about never facing hardships, but about maintaining determination and progress even when times are tough. Success comes from the capacity to rise and move forward after being knocked down.

"YOUR FUTURE HASN'T BEEN WRITTEN YET. NO ONE'S HAS. YOUR FUTURE IS WHATEVER YOU MAKE IT. SO MAKE IT A GOOD ONE."

MEANING:

This quote emphasizes the power of free will and personal responsibility in shaping your future. It suggests that the future is not predetermined and that you have the ability to create your own path. By making conscious choices and taking positive actions, you can influence the course of your life. It encourages taking control of your destiny and striving to make it meaningful and fulfilling.

"AFTER ALL, TOMORROW IS ANOTHER DAY!"

GONE WITH THE WIND

MEANING:

This quote offers a message of hope and renewal. No matter how difficult today may be, tomorrow provides a fresh start and new opportunities. It encourages looking forward with optimism and not being weighed down by present troubles. This perspective helps in maintaining a positive outlook and resilience in the face of challenges.

MEANING:

This quote highlights the importance of laughter and humor as coping mechanisms. In difficult times, laughter can provide relief, foster resilience, and bring people together. It can be a powerful tool to lighten the mood and maintain a positive outlook. Sometimes, humor is the best way to deal with life's challenges and find strength.

MEANING:

This quote speaks to the bravery required to acknowledge the world's imperfections and still find beauty and love in it. It suggests that true courage involves accepting reality with all its flaws and choosing to embrace it despite its imperfections. Loving the world in its entirety, including the good and the bad, reflects deep strength and acceptance. This perspective allows for a more compassionate and realistic appreciation of life.

"THE GREATEST GLORY IN LIVING LIES NOT IN NEVER FALLING, BUT IN RISING EVERY TIME WE FALL."

INVICTUS

MEANING:

This quote underscores the value of resilience and persistence. True success and honor come not from avoiding failure, but from recovering and rising after setbacks. Falling is a natural part of life, but the ability to get back up and continue striving defines true strength and character. It highlights the importance of perseverance in achieving lasting success.

MEANING:

This quote expresses a moment of ultimate triumph and exhilaration. It symbolizes a feeling of being on top of the world, often experienced during a significant personal achievement or joyful event. This declaration of exuberance reflects confidence, empowerment, and the sense of being unstoppable. It captures a peak moment of pride and fulfillment.

"OUR GREATEST GLORY IS NOT IN NEVER FALLING, BUT IN RISING EVERY TIME WE FALL."

MEANING:

This quote reiterates the idea that true achievement is demonstrated through resilience. The focus is not on avoiding failure, but on the ability to recover and continue after experiencing setbacks. Rising after a fall showcases inner strength and determination. It's a reminder that persistence and the courage to try again are what lead to eventual success.

"SOME PEOPLE CAN'T BELIEVE IN THEMSELVES UNTIL SOMEONE ELSE BELIEVES IN THEM FIRST."

GOOD WILL HUNTING

MEANING:

This quote highlights the impact of external validation on self-belief. For many, confidence and self-worth are bolstered by the support and belief of others. Encouragement and affirmation from others can be crucial in helping individuals recognize their own potential. It underscores the importance of providing support and belief in others to help them achieve their goals.

MEANING:

The quote emphasizes the significance of self-awareness and self-acceptance in uncovering one's authentic power. It motivates individuals to ponder on their distinct qualities, talents, and sense of self. By acknowledging and embracing their uniqueness, individuals can unlock their complete capabilities. The quote implies that genuine strength comes from embracing one's true self, rather than emulating others, to become the best version of oneself.

"YOU'VE GOT TO ASK YOURSELF ONE QUESTION: 'DO I FEEL LUCKY?' WELL, DO YA, PUNK?"

DIRTY HARRY

MEANING:

This quote, often associated with a challenge or confrontation, underscores self-reflection and confidence. It suggests considering your own position and readiness before taking action. Feeling 'lucky' implies confidence and readiness to face challenges. It's a provocative prompt to assess one's own capabilities and resolve.

MEANING:

This quote highlights the importance of authenticity and self-fulfillment. Living according to others' expectations can lead to personal dissatisfaction. It suggests prioritizing your own needs and values, even if it means difficult choices. True happiness and integrity come from living a life true to oneself.

"THE FUTURE BELONGS TO THOSE WHO BELIEVE IN THE BEAUTY OF THEIR DREAMS."

THE PRINCESS DIARIES

MEANING:

This quote emphasizes the power of belief in shaping the future. Dreams and aspirations are the foundation of future achievements. Believing in the value and possibility of your dreams motivates action and perseverance. It encourages maintaining faith in your vision to create a fulfilling future.

> ## "JUST BECAUSE SOMEONE STUMBLES AND LOSES THEIR PATH, DOESN'T MEAN THEY'RE LOST FOREVER."

MEANING:

This quote offers hope and redemption. Making mistakes or experiencing setbacks does not define a person's future. It's possible to recover, find direction, and succeed despite past errors. It emphasizes the potential for growth and change, suggesting that setbacks are temporary and can be overcome.

"THE TRUTH IS, EVERYONE IS GOING TO HURT YOU. YOU JUST GOT TO FIND THE ONES WORTH SUFFERING FOR."

THE PURSUIT OF HAPPYNESS

MEANING:

This quote acknowledges that pain and disappointment are inevitable parts of relationships. It suggests that instead of trying to avoid all hurt, we should seek relationships with people who are worth enduring pain for. These are the people whose presence and love bring enough joy and meaning to outweigh the inevitable challenges. It speaks to the idea that deep, meaningful connections come with both highs and lows.

MEANING:

This quote highlights the unchangeable nature of the past and the potential we have to influence our future. It encourages letting go of regrets and focusing on what can be done now to create a better tomorrow. By accepting that the past is fixed, we can direct our energy towards actions that will shape a more positive and fulfilling future. It emphasizes the power of forward-thinking and personal agency.

MEANING:

This quote encourages individuality and self-expression. It suggests that societal expectations or others' opinions should not dictate how we live our lives. Embracing our true selves and being authentic allows us to lead more fulfilling and genuine lives. It's a call to resist conformity and celebrate our unique identities.

"WE'RE ALL STORIES IN THE END. JUST MAKE IT A GOOD ONE, EH?"

MEANING:

This quote reflects on the transient nature of life and the legacy we leave behind. It suggests that our lives are like stories, and it's up to us to make them meaningful and memorable. By living with intention and purpose, we can create a "good" story that others will remember and be inspired by. It encourages living a life that is rich with experiences and positive impact.

> # "IN EVERY JOB THAT MUST BE DONE, THERE IS AN ELEMENT OF FUN."

MARY POPPINS

MEANING:

This quote suggests that even in tasks that are necessary and perhaps mundane, there is potential to find enjoyment. By approaching our work with a positive attitude, we can uncover the fun aspects and make the experience more pleasant. It encourages finding joy and satisfaction in all activities, even those that are routine or challenging. It's a reminder to seek out the lighter side of life's responsibilities.

MERIDA (VOICED BY KELLY MACDONALD)

"YOU CONTROL YOUR DESTINY — YOU DON'T NEED MAGIC TO DO IT. AND THERE ARE NO MAGICAL SHORTCUTS TO SOLVING YOUR PROBLEMS."

BRAVE

MEANING:

This quote emphasizes personal responsibility and effort in shaping our lives. It suggests that we have the power to influence our destiny through our actions and decisions. There are no easy fixes or magical solutions; instead, success and problem-solving come from hard work and perseverance. It encourages self-reliance and determination in pursuing our goals.

"THE FLOWER THAT BLOOMS IN ADVERSITY IS THE MOST RARE AND BEAUTIFUL OF ALL."

MULAN

MEANING:

This quote suggests that the most remarkable growth and beauty often emerge from difficult circumstances. Adversity can foster resilience, strength, and unique qualities that make one stand out. It highlights the value of overcoming challenges and how they contribute to personal development and character. It's a celebration of the strength and beauty found in those who thrive despite hardship.

MEANING:

This quote uses the metaphor of riding a bicycle to illustrate the importance of continual progress in life. Just as a bicycle stays upright as long as it's moving, our lives require constant forward motion to maintain balance and stability. It encourages persistence and the idea that even small, steady progress is crucial to keeping life on track. It suggests that stagnation can lead to imbalance and instability.

MEANING:

This quote emphasizes the value of consistent effort over the pursuit of perfection. It suggests that real change and growth come from daily dedication and hard work. Perfection is an unattainable ideal, but effort is something within everyone's reach. It encourages focusing on continuous improvement and the importance of persistence in achieving transformation.

"YOU DON'T HAVE TO BE PERFECT TO BE AMAZING."

DOLLY PARTON'S COAT OF MANY COLORS

MEANING:

This quote reassures that excellence and worth are not contingent on perfection. Everyone has unique strengths and qualities that make them amazing, even with imperfections. It encourages self-acceptance and recognizing one's own value despite flaws. It's a reminder that striving for perfection can be a barrier to appreciating and celebrating one's true self.

"BELIEVE IN YOURSELVES. DREAM. TRY. DO GOOD."

MEANING:

This quote encourages self-belief, aspiration, effort, and ethical behavior. It suggests that having faith in oneself is the foundation for dreaming big and taking action. Trying your best and striving to do good in the world are key components of a fulfilling life. It's a call to combine personal ambition with integrity and kindness.

"THE FUTURE IS SOMETHING WHICH EVERYONE REACHES AT THE RATE OF 60 MINUTES AN HOUR, WHATEVER HE DOES, WHOEVER HE IS."

SHADOWLANDS

MEANING:

This quote highlights the uniform passage of time for everyone, regardless of their actions or identity. It suggests that time is a constant and equalizing factor in life. The way we choose to spend our time is what differentiates our experiences and achievements. It's a reminder to make the most of the time we have, as it passes at the same rate for everyone.

"IT'S NOT WHAT I AM UNDERNEATH, BUT WHAT I DO THAT DEFINES ME."

MEANING:

This quote highlights the importance of actions over inherent qualities or internal intentions. It suggests that our true character is revealed through our behavior and choices. People are judged by their actions, which have a tangible impact, rather than their hidden qualities or thoughts. It emphasizes the value of outward conduct and tangible contributions.

"LIFE'S NOT ABOUT HOW HARD OF A HIT YOU CAN GIVE... IT'S ABOUT HOW MANY YOU CAN TAKE AND KEEP MOVING FORWARD."

ROCKY BALBOA

MEANING:

This quote emphasizes resilience and endurance over aggression or strength. It suggests that the true measure of character is not in how much you can dish out, but in how well you can withstand adversity and keep going. It celebrates the ability to endure difficulties and maintain forward momentum. It's a call to persist and remain strong in the face of challenges.

MEANING:

This quote uses the metaphor of sailing to illustrate adaptability and resourcefulness. It suggests that while we cannot control external circumstances, we can adjust our actions and strategies to navigate through them. It emphasizes the importance of flexibility and proactive problem-solving in achieving goals. It's a reminder that success often comes from how we respond to challenges, rather than the absence of challenges.

"SOMETIMES THE RIGHT PATH IS NOT THE EASIEST ONE."

MEANING:

This quote suggests that doing what is right often requires effort, sacrifice, and resilience. The best decisions and actions may involve facing challenges and enduring hardships. It implies that the value and rewards of the right path come from the growth and lessons learned along the way. This quote encourages perseverance and integrity, even when the journey is tough.

MEANING:

This quote emphasizes the long-lasting impact of our actions and decisions. It suggests that our deeds leave a legacy that can influence the future and be remembered long after we are gone. Every choice we make contributes to a larger narrative that shapes history and affects others. It encourages living a life of purpose and significance, knowing that our actions have enduring consequences.

"THE NIGHT IS DARKEST JUST BEFORE THE DAWN. AND I PROMISE YOU, THE DAWN IS COMING."

THE DARK KNIGHT

MEANING:

This quote offers hope and reassurance during difficult times. It acknowledges that moments of despair often precede breakthroughs and new beginnings. The promise of dawn symbolizes the certainty of positive change and the end of hardship. It encourages patience and faith, reminding us that brighter times are ahead.

"IT'S NOT WHETHER YOU GET KNOCKED DOWN, IT'S WHETHER YOU GET UP."

ROCKY BALBOA

MEANING:

This quote focuses on resilience and the importance of recovery after setbacks. Everyone faces difficulties and failures, but true strength lies in the ability to rise again. It encourages perseverance and a determined spirit, suggesting that how we respond to challenges defines our character and success. The act of getting up and trying again is what ultimately leads to achievement.

MEANING:

This quote underscores the importance of dreams and aspirations in shaping the future. Believing in the value and potential of one's dreams is crucial for taking action and making them a reality. It suggests that those who have faith in their vision and work towards it are the ones who create a meaningful and fulfilling future. This belief fuels motivation and persistence.

"THE GREATEST THING YOU'LL EVER LEARN IS JUST TO LOVE AND BE LOVED IN RETURN."

MEANING:

This quote emphasizes the fundamental importance of love in life. It suggests that giving and receiving love is the most valuable and profound experience one can have. Love enriches life, brings happiness, and fosters deep connections with others. Learning to love and be loved is seen as the ultimate lesson and source of fulfillment.

"YOU'RE NOT OBLIGATED TO WIN. YOU'RE OBLIGATED TO KEEP TRYING. TO THE BEST YOU CAN DO EVERY DAY."

JOY

MEANING:

This quote emphasizes the importance of effort and perseverance over immediate success. The focus is on continuous improvement and giving your best effort regardless of the outcome. It suggests that persistence and dedication are more important than winning or achieving perfection. This mindset encourages resilience and a strong work ethic.

"IT TAKES GREAT COURAGE TO SEE THE WORLD IN ALL ITS TAINTED GLORY, AND STILL TO LOVE IT."

MEANING:

This quote speaks to the bravery required to acknowledge the world's imperfections and still find beauty and love in it. It suggests that true courage involves accepting reality with all its flaws and choosing to embrace it despite its imperfections. Loving the world in its entirety, including the good and the bad, reflects deep strength and acceptance. This perspective allows for a more compassionate and realistic appreciation of life.

MEANING:

This quote emphasizes the importance of present actions in shaping the future. It suggests that immediate decisions and efforts have a significant impact on outcomes. Taking action in the present moment is crucial for achieving goals and making progress. This perspective encourages proactive behavior and seizing opportunities without delay.

TOM HARDY

"YOU MUSTN'T BE AFRAID TO DREAM A LITTLE BIGGER, DARLING."

INCEPTION

MEANING:

This quote encourages breaking free from limitations and aiming higher with your aspirations. It suggests that fear should not restrict the scope of your dreams. Dreaming big requires courage and an open mind to envision possibilities beyond the ordinary. By dreaming bigger, you allow yourself to achieve greater things and expand your potential.

"YOU EITHER DIE A HERO, OR YOU LIVE LONG ENOUGH TO SEE YOURSELF BECOME THE VILLAIN."

MEANING:

This quote explores the idea of legacy and the potential for one's character to change over time. It suggests that maintaining heroism and integrity can be challenging over a prolonged period. If one's journey continues long enough, they may face situations that could compromise their values or turn them into a villain. It highlights the complexity of human nature and the importance of staying true to one's principles.

"YOU CONTROL YOUR DESTINY — YOU DON'T NEED MAGIC TO DO IT. AND THERE ARE NO MAGICAL SHORTCUTS TO SOLVING YOUR PROBLEMS."

BRAVE

MEANING:

This quote emphasizes personal responsibility and the power of self-determination. It suggests that achieving goals and overcoming challenges requires effort and perseverance rather than relying on external forces or quick fixes. Taking control of your own path and working diligently are essential for success. This perspective encourages a proactive and realistic approach to life.

MEANING:

This quote emphasizes the quality of experiences over the mere passage of time. Life's value is measured by memorable and impactful moments rather than the number of days lived. These extraordinary experiences bring joy, wonder, and meaning to life. It encourages seeking out and cherishing moments that leave a lasting impression and bring profound happiness.

THANK YOU FOR PURCHASING THIS BOOK